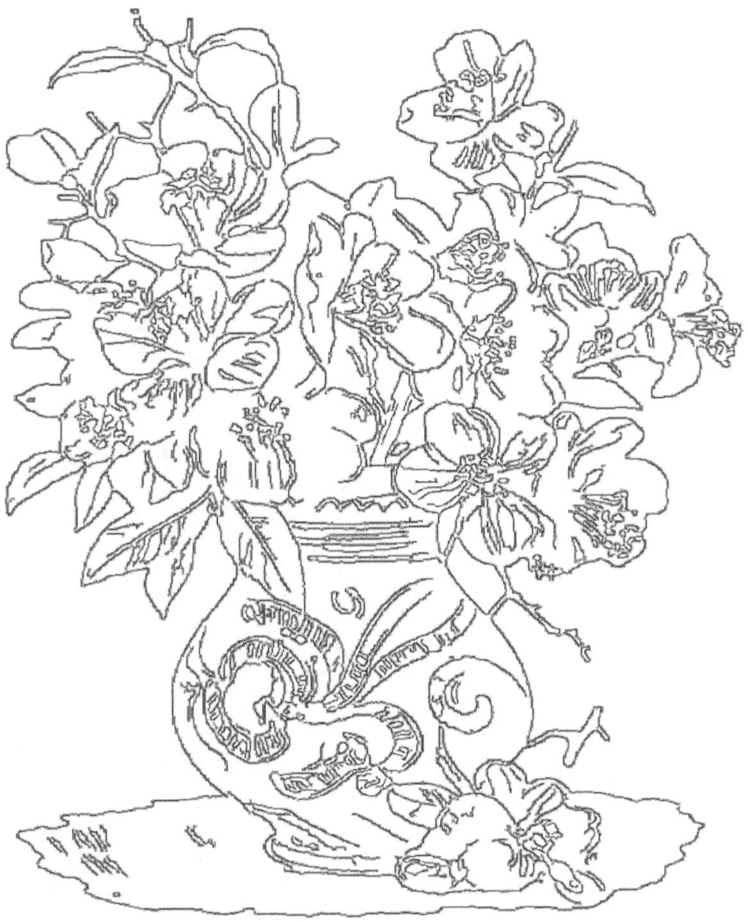

Enjoy Coloring !!!

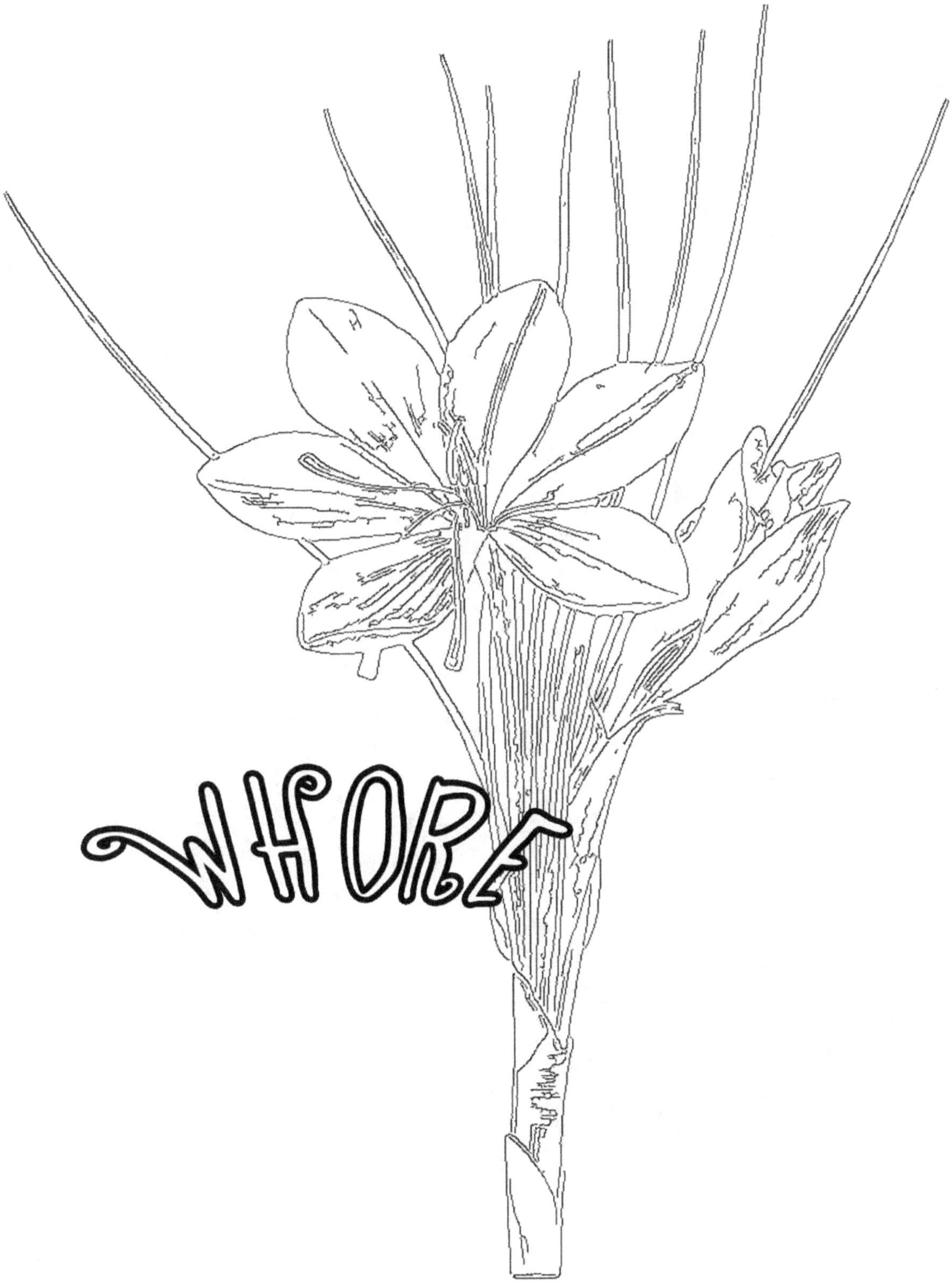
WHORE

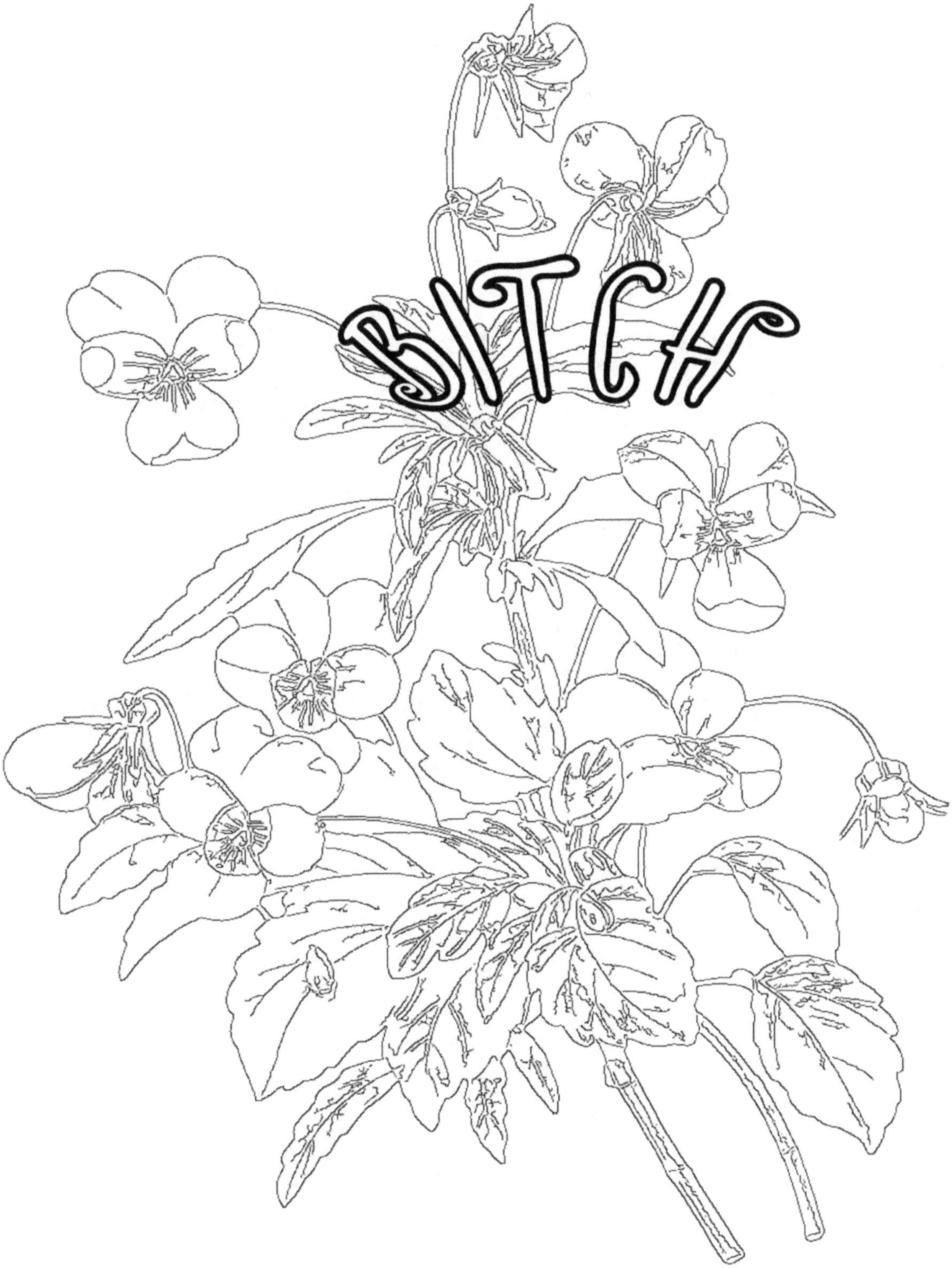
BITCH

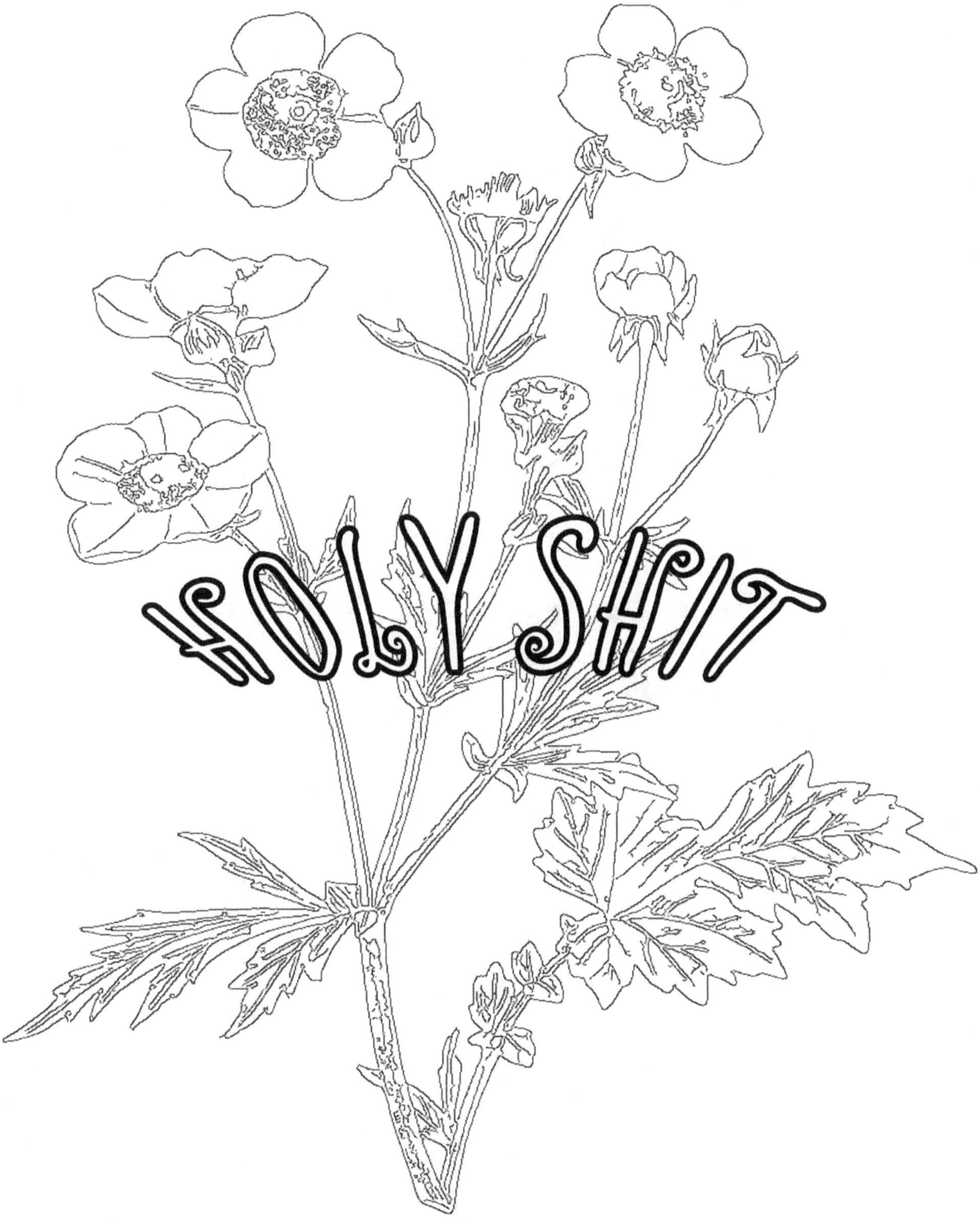
HOLY SHIT

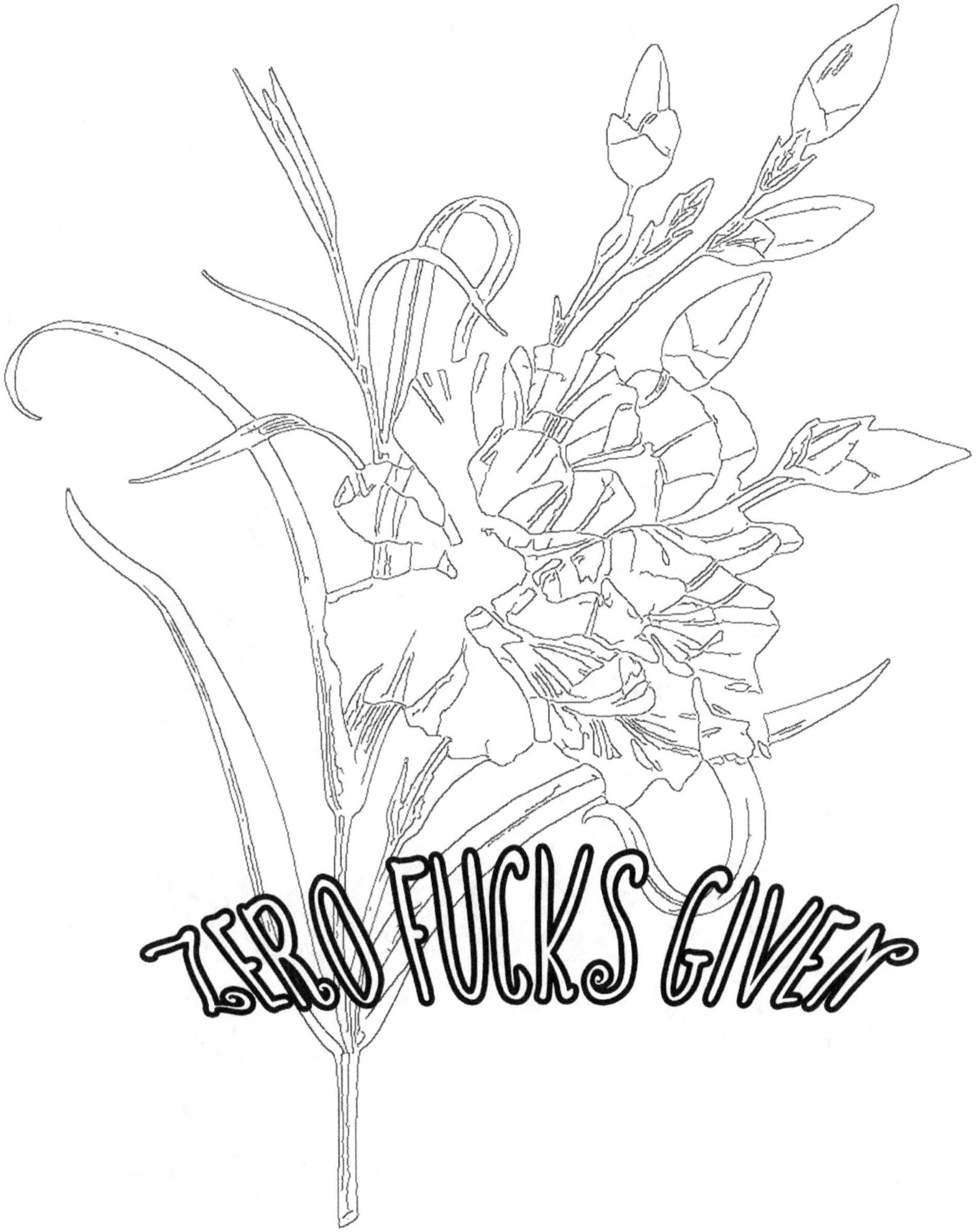
ZERO FUCKS GIVEN

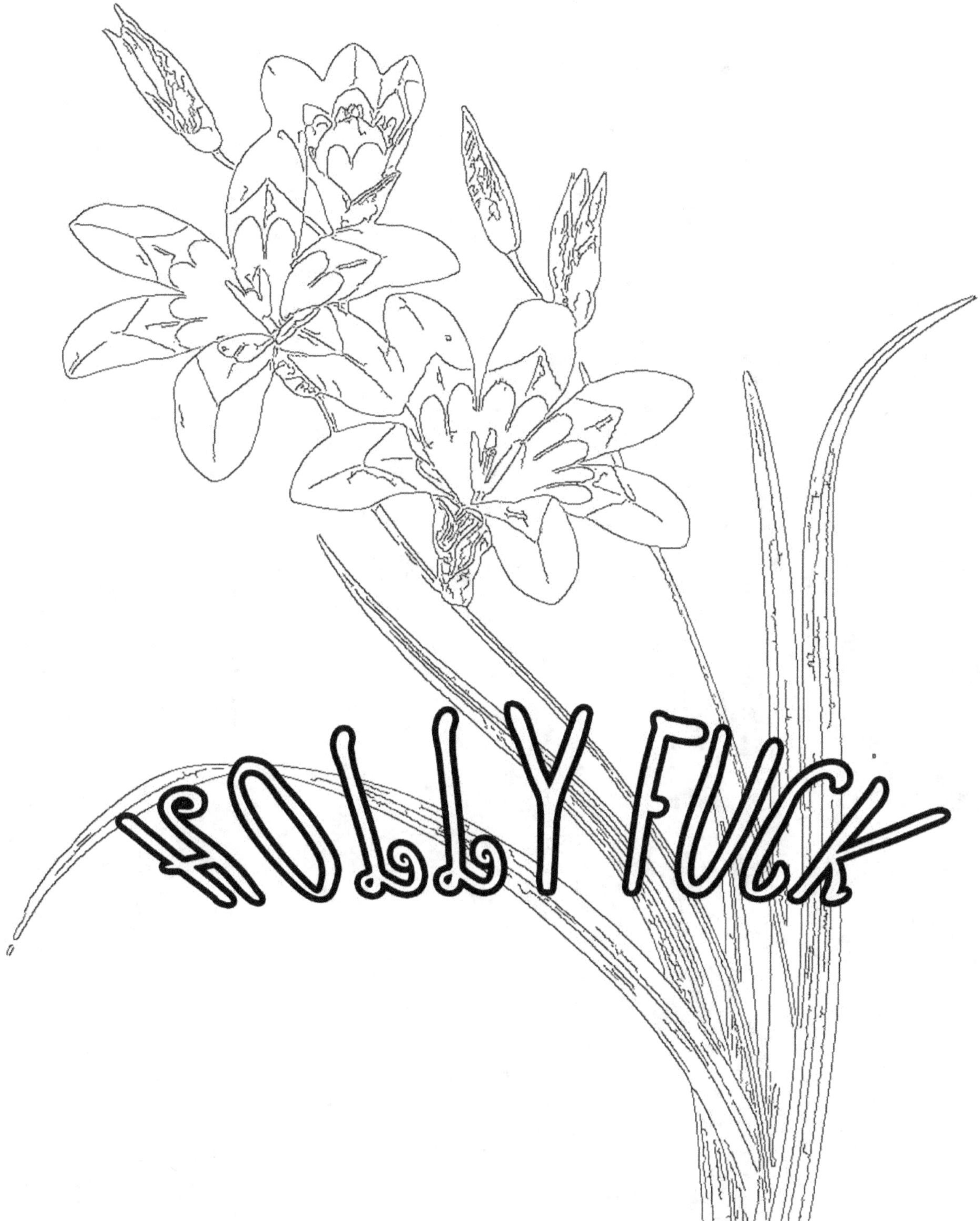
HOLLY FUCK

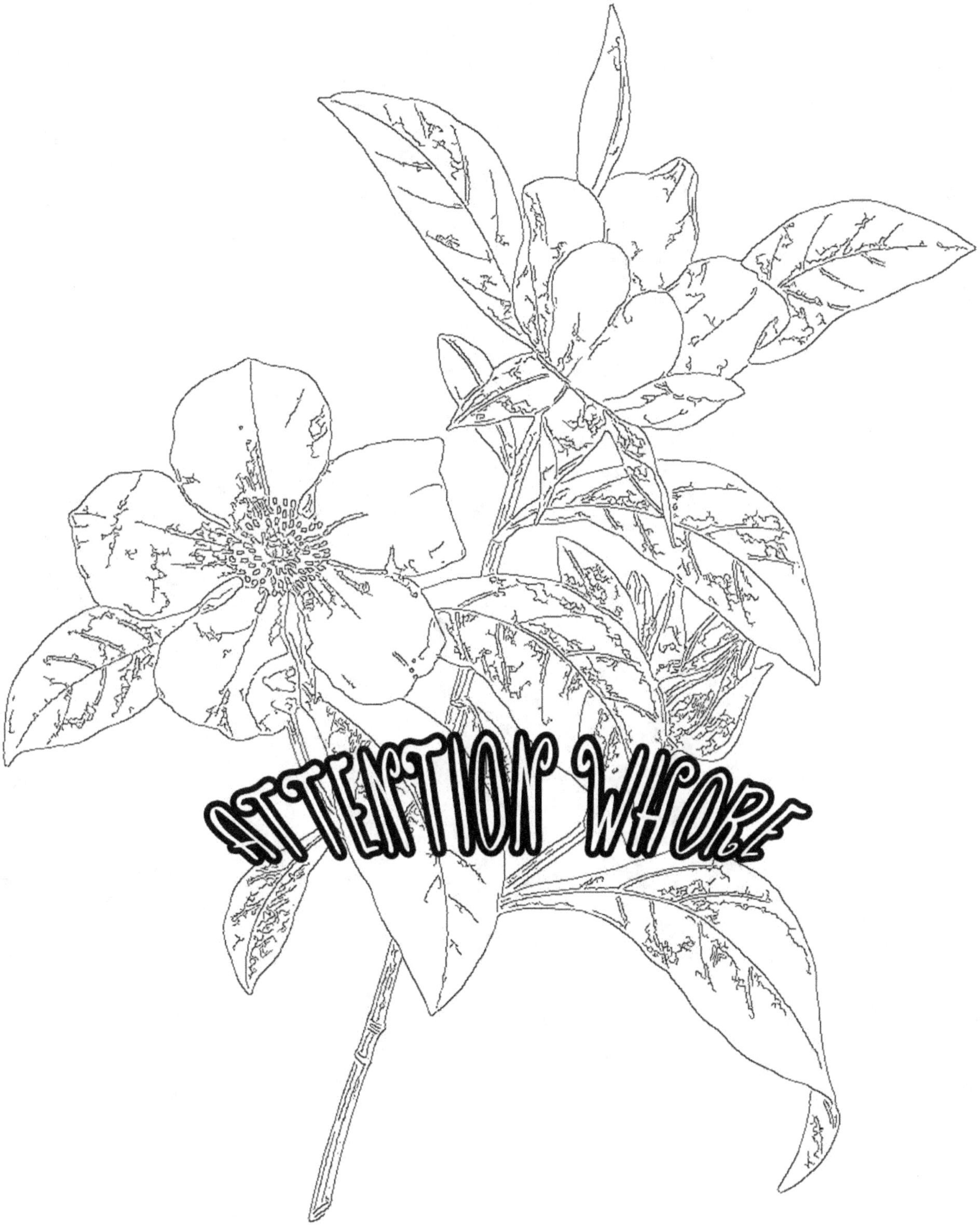
ATTENTION WHORE

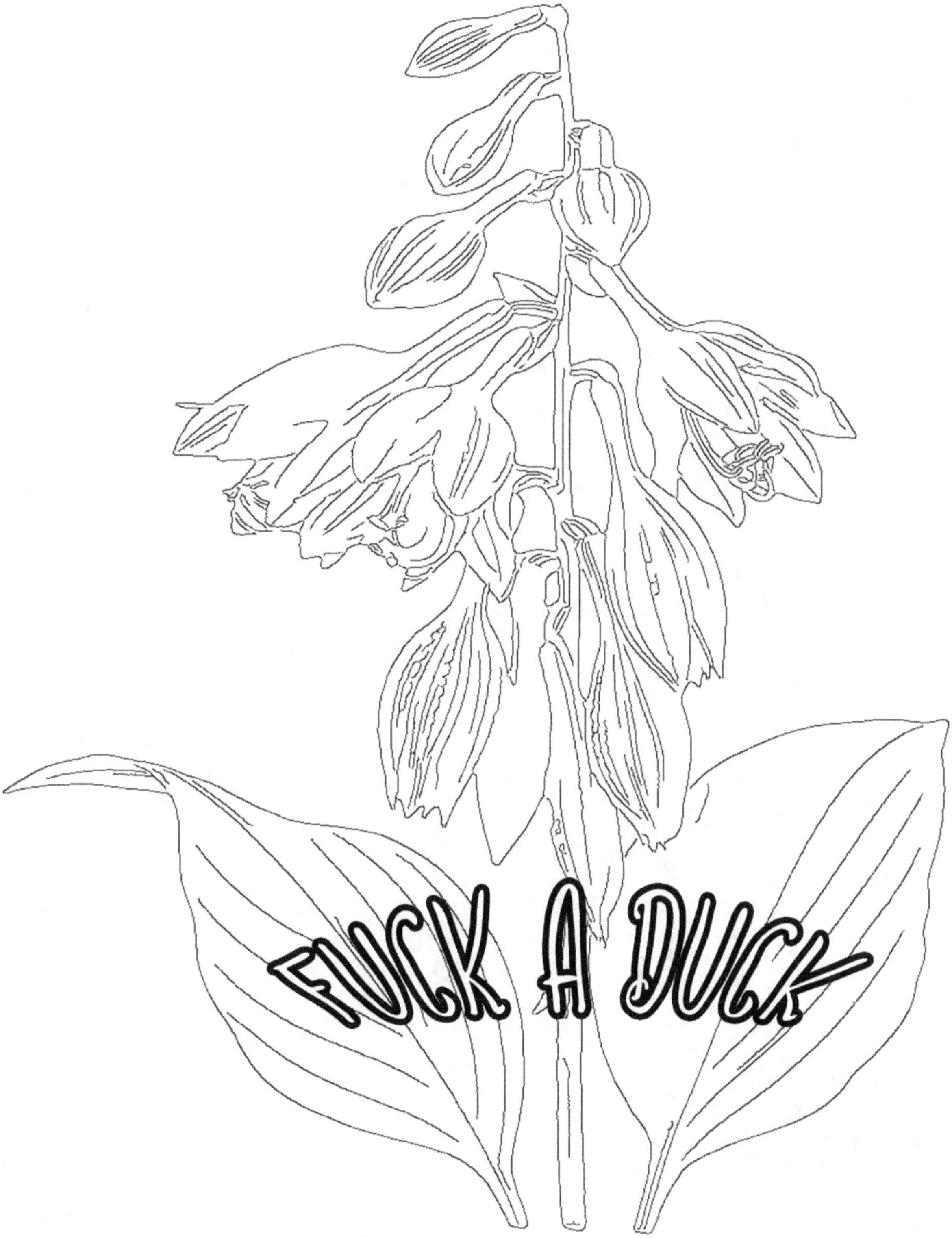
FUCK A DUCK

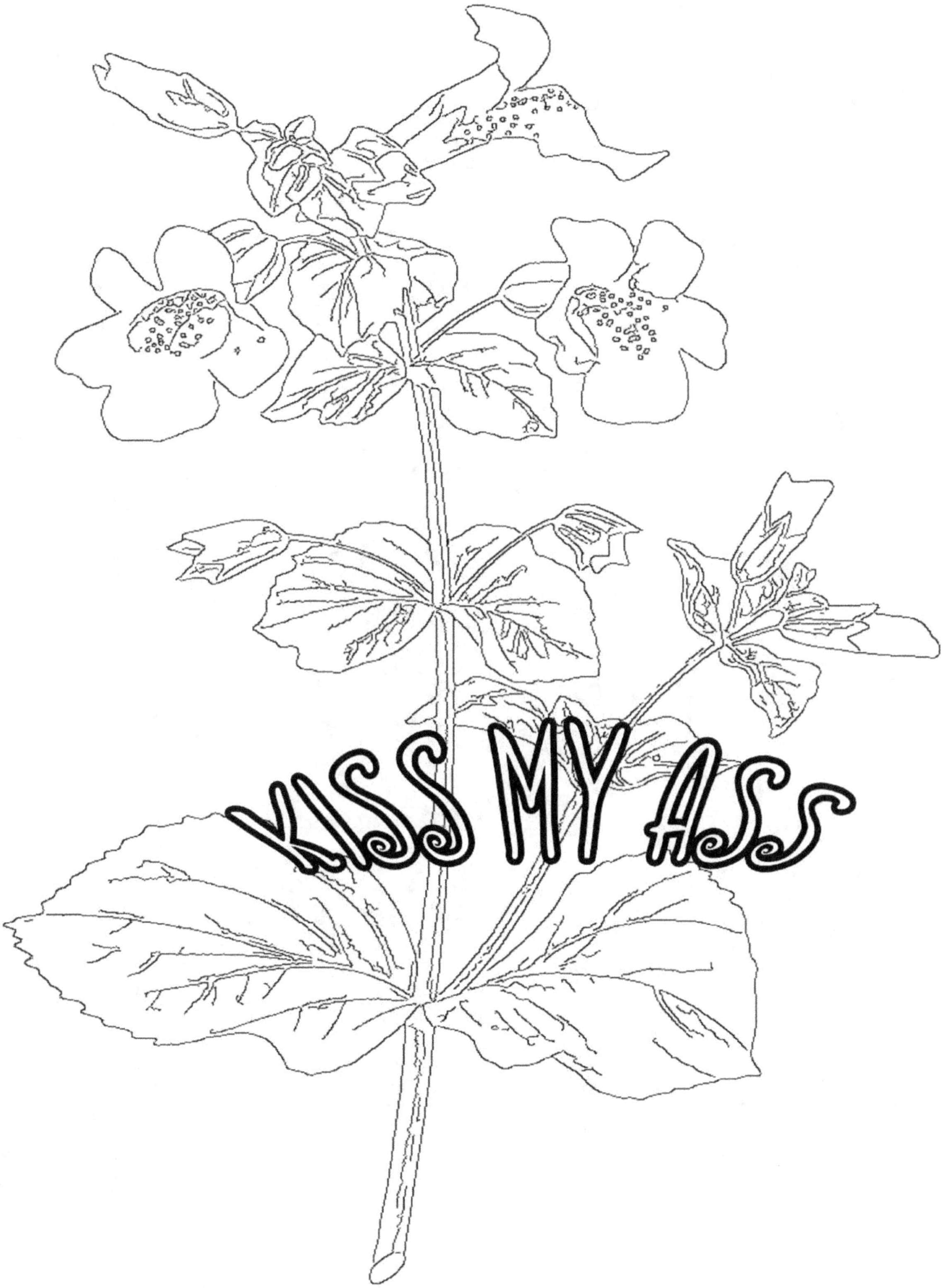
KISS MY ASS

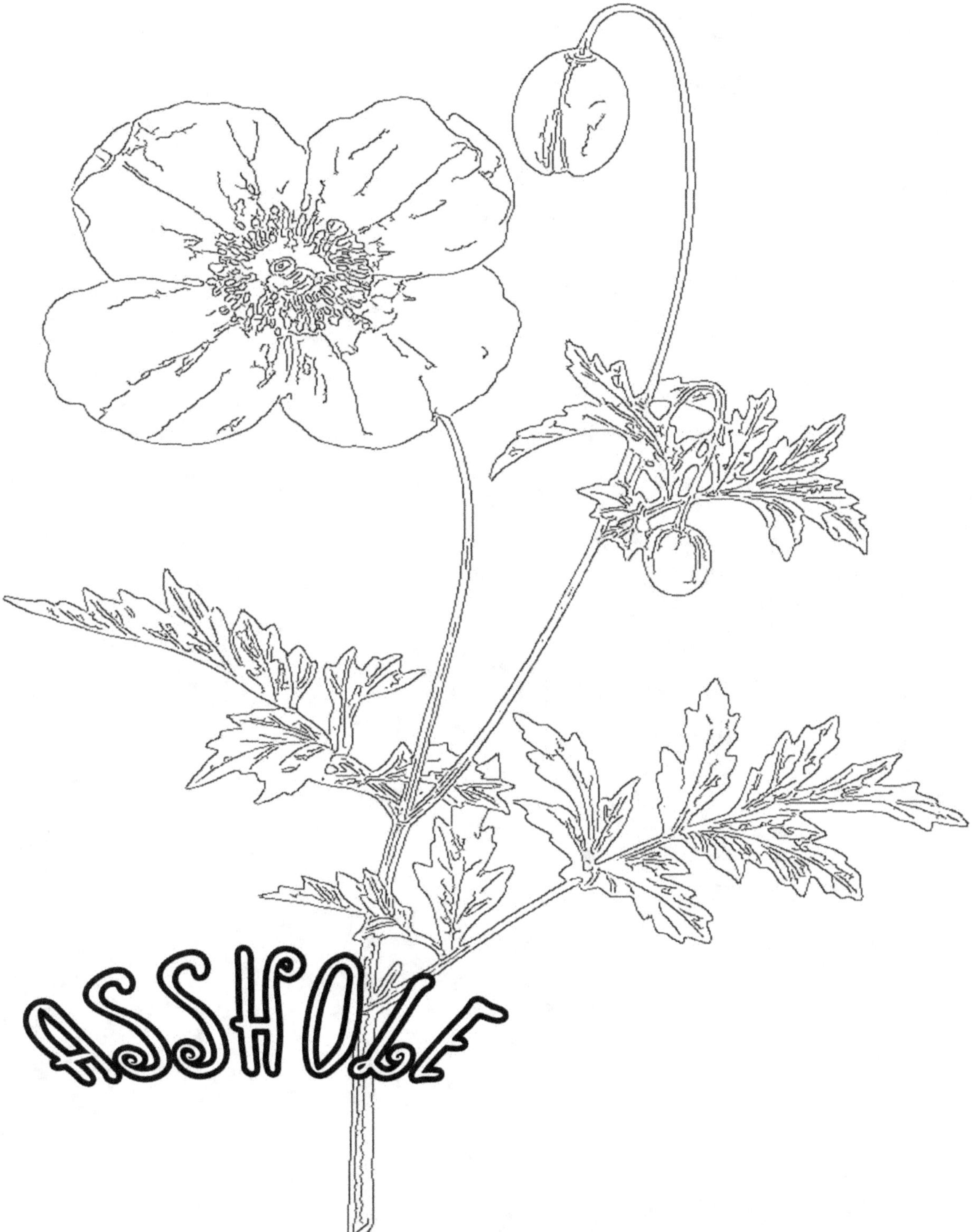
ASSHOLE

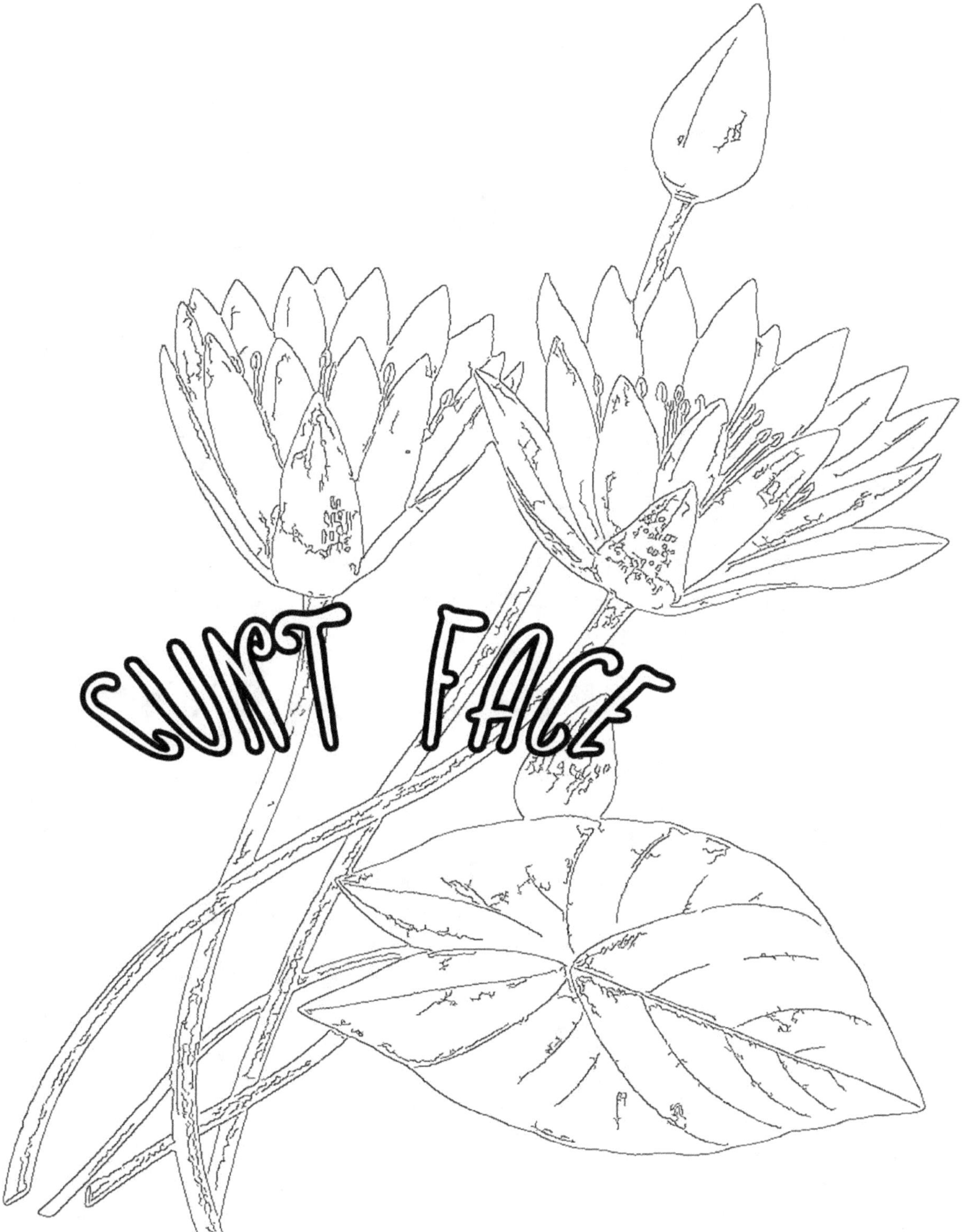
CUNT FACE

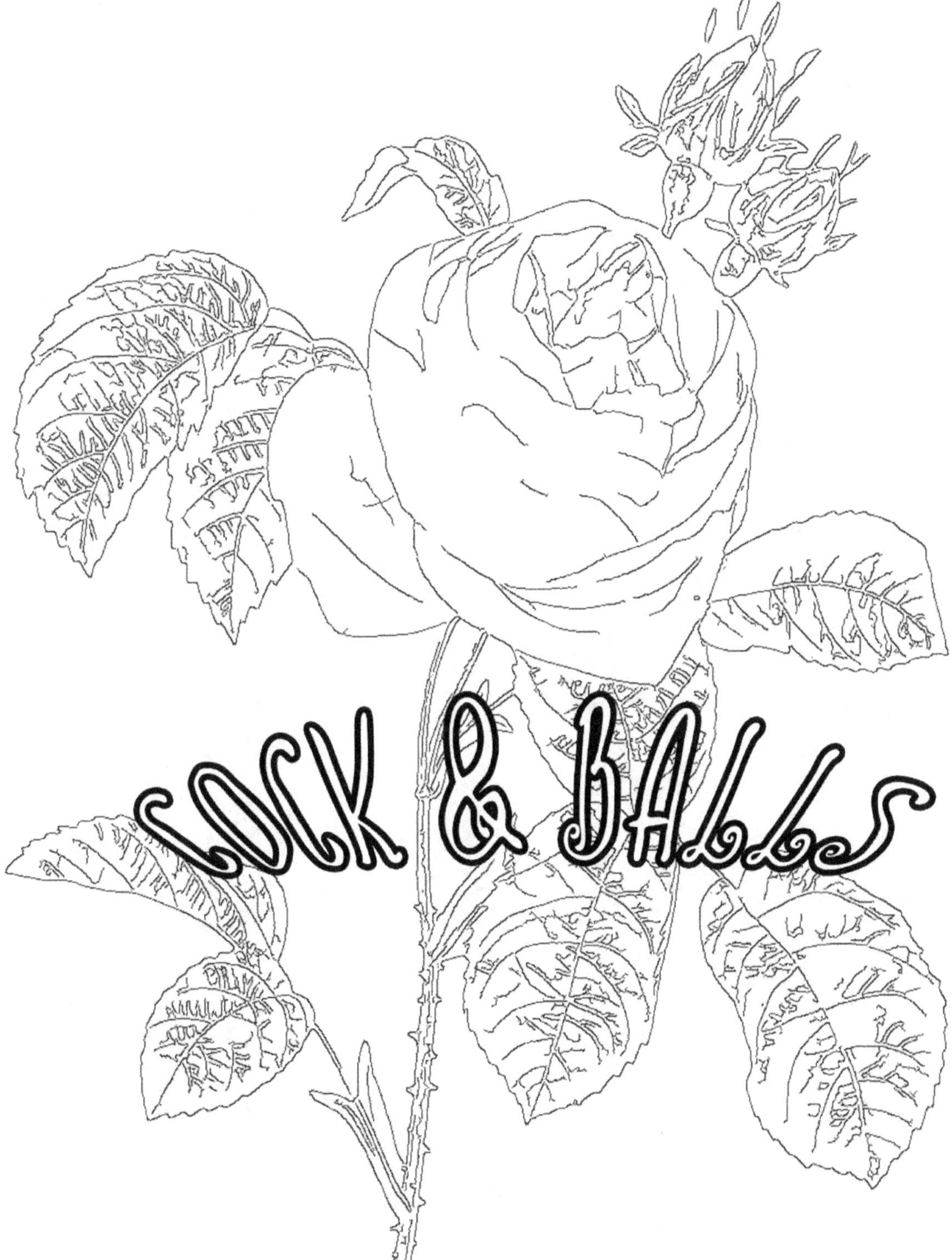
COCK & BALLS

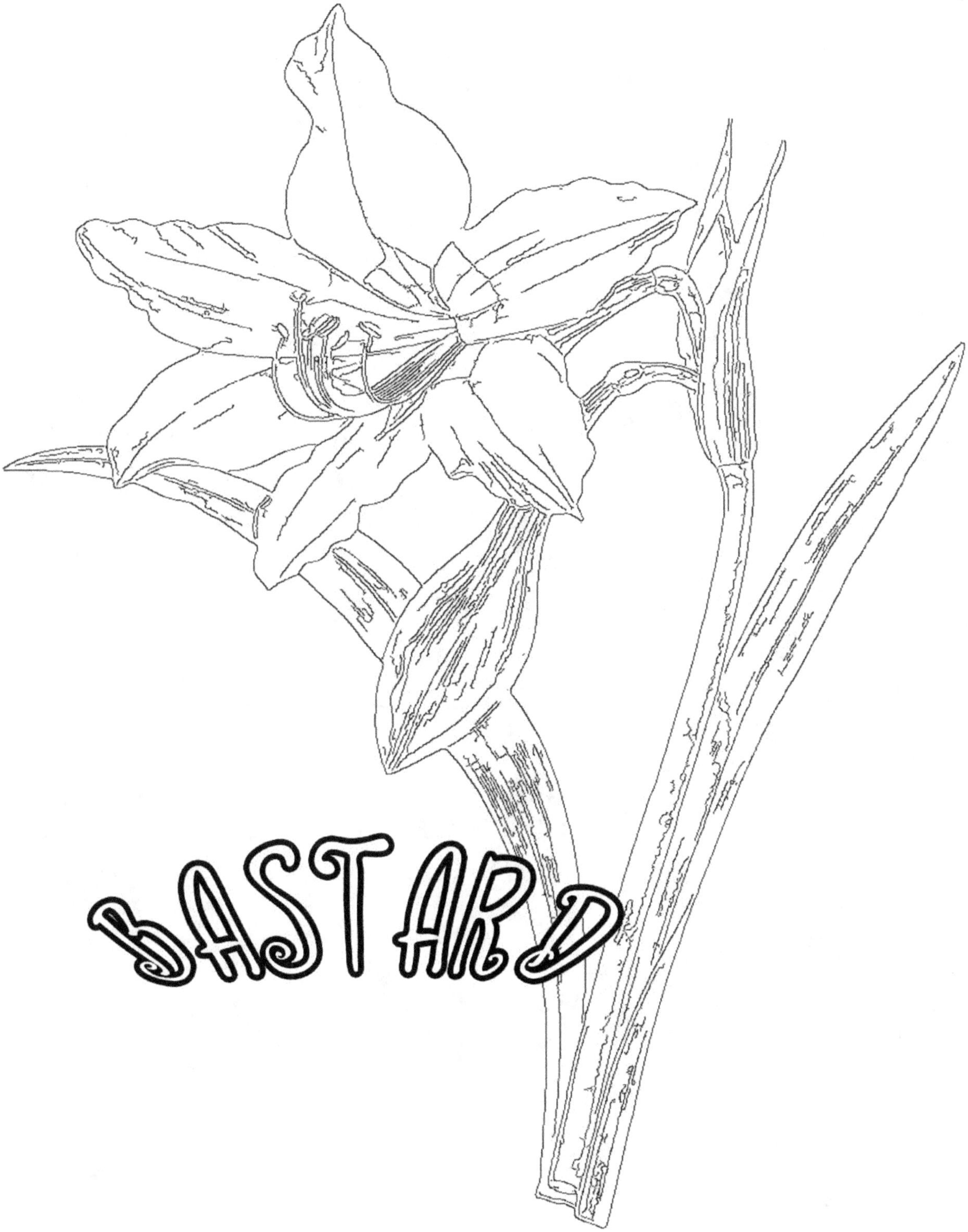
BASTARD

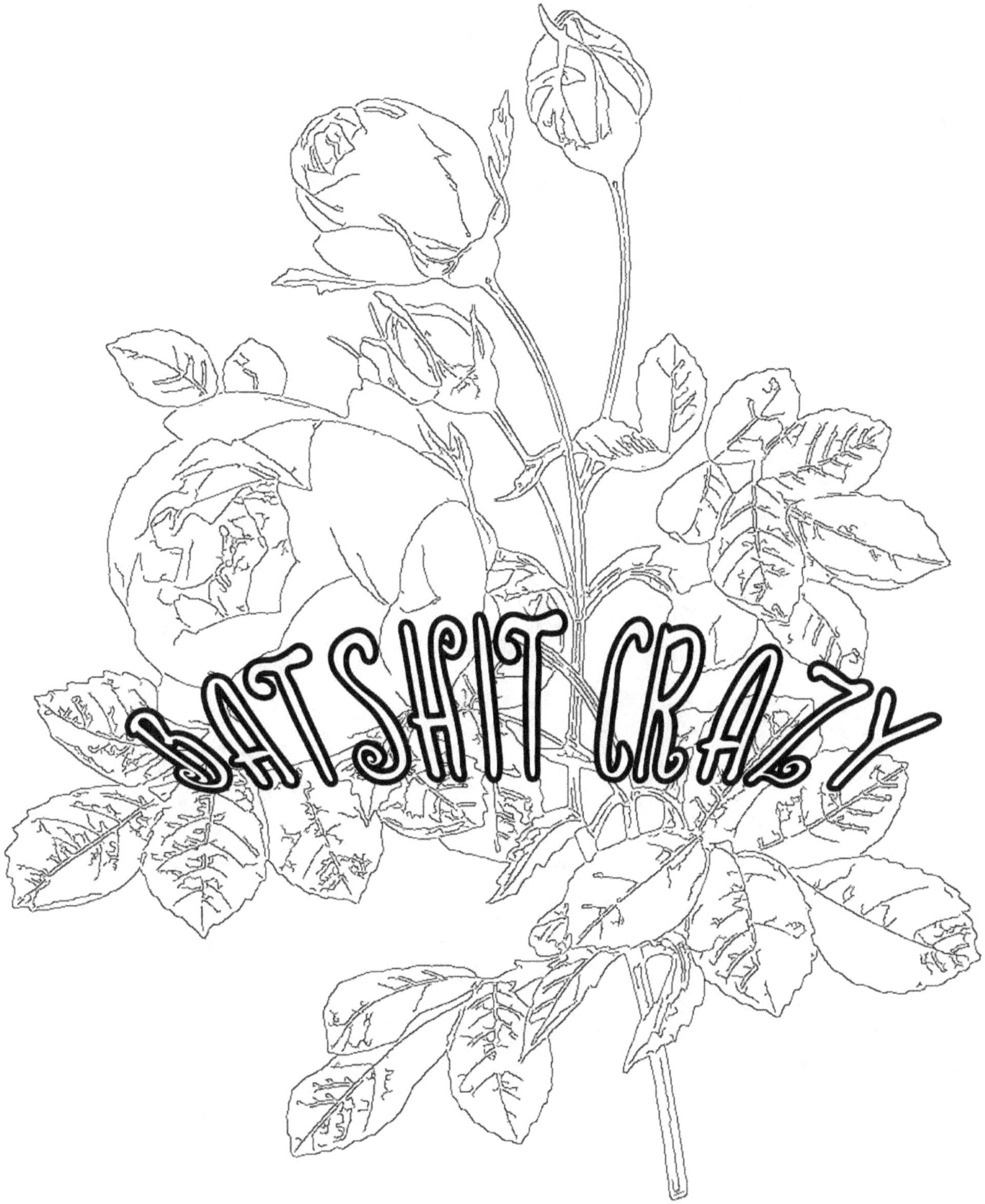
BATSHIT CRAZY

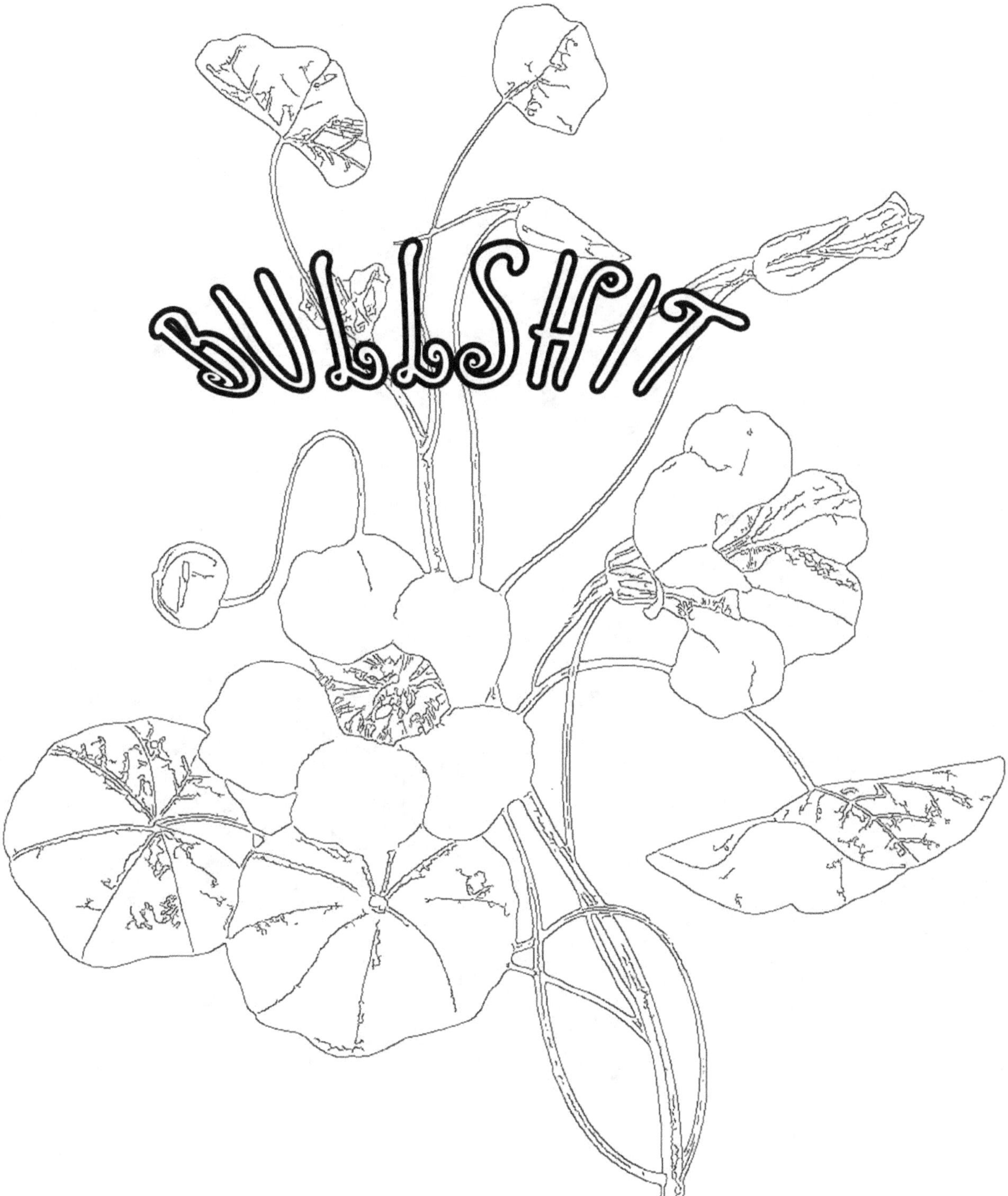
BULLSHIT

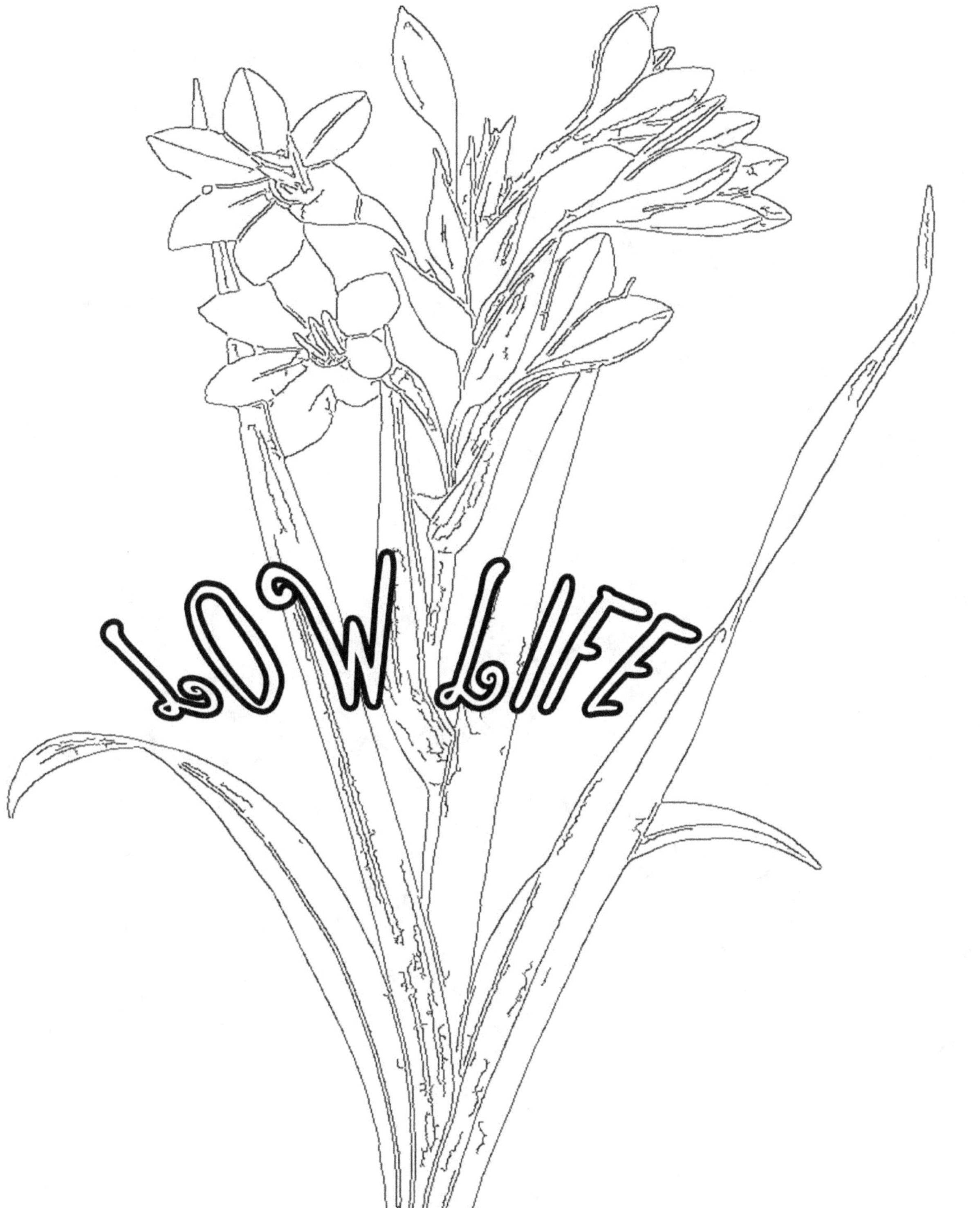
LOW LIFE

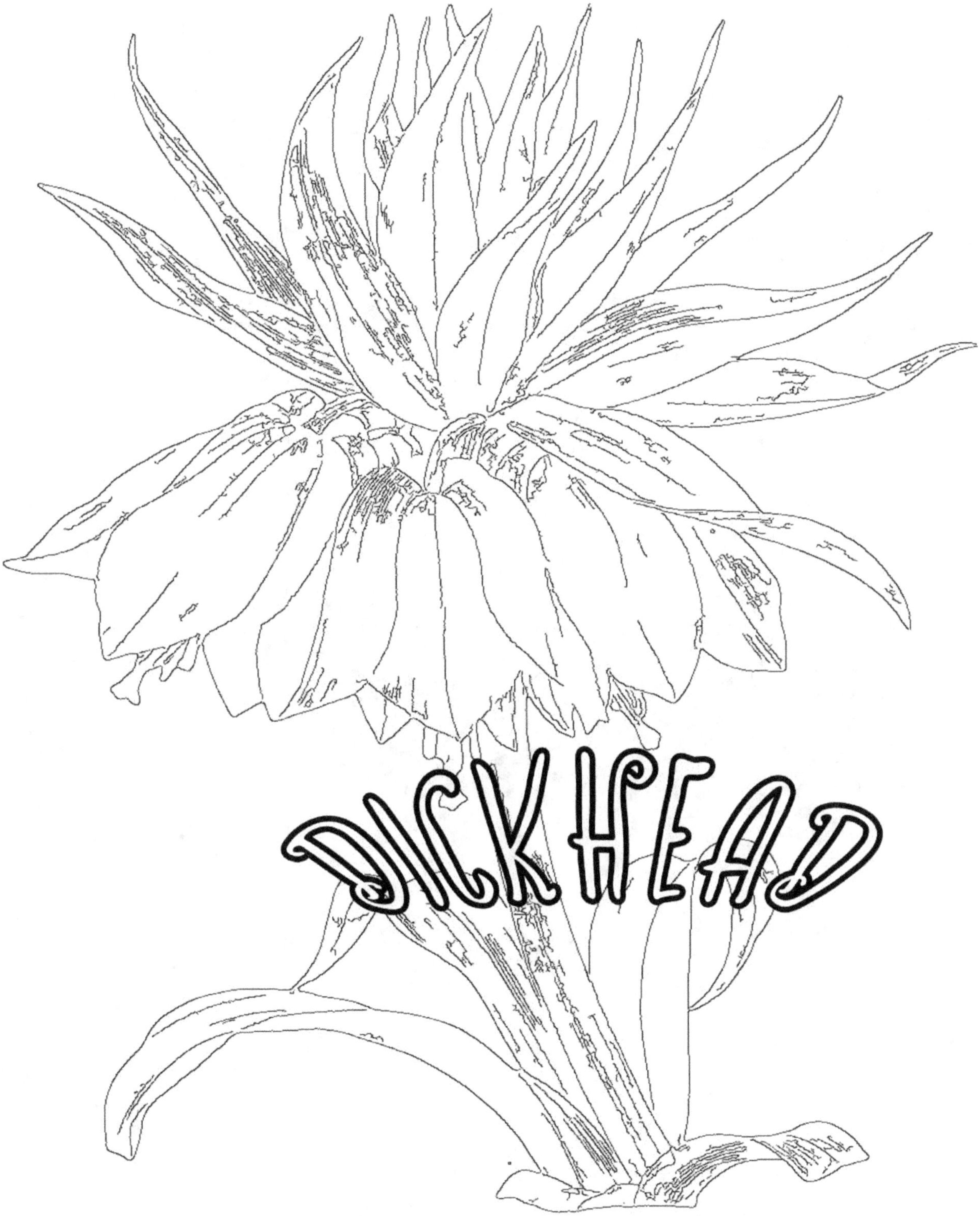
DICKHEAD

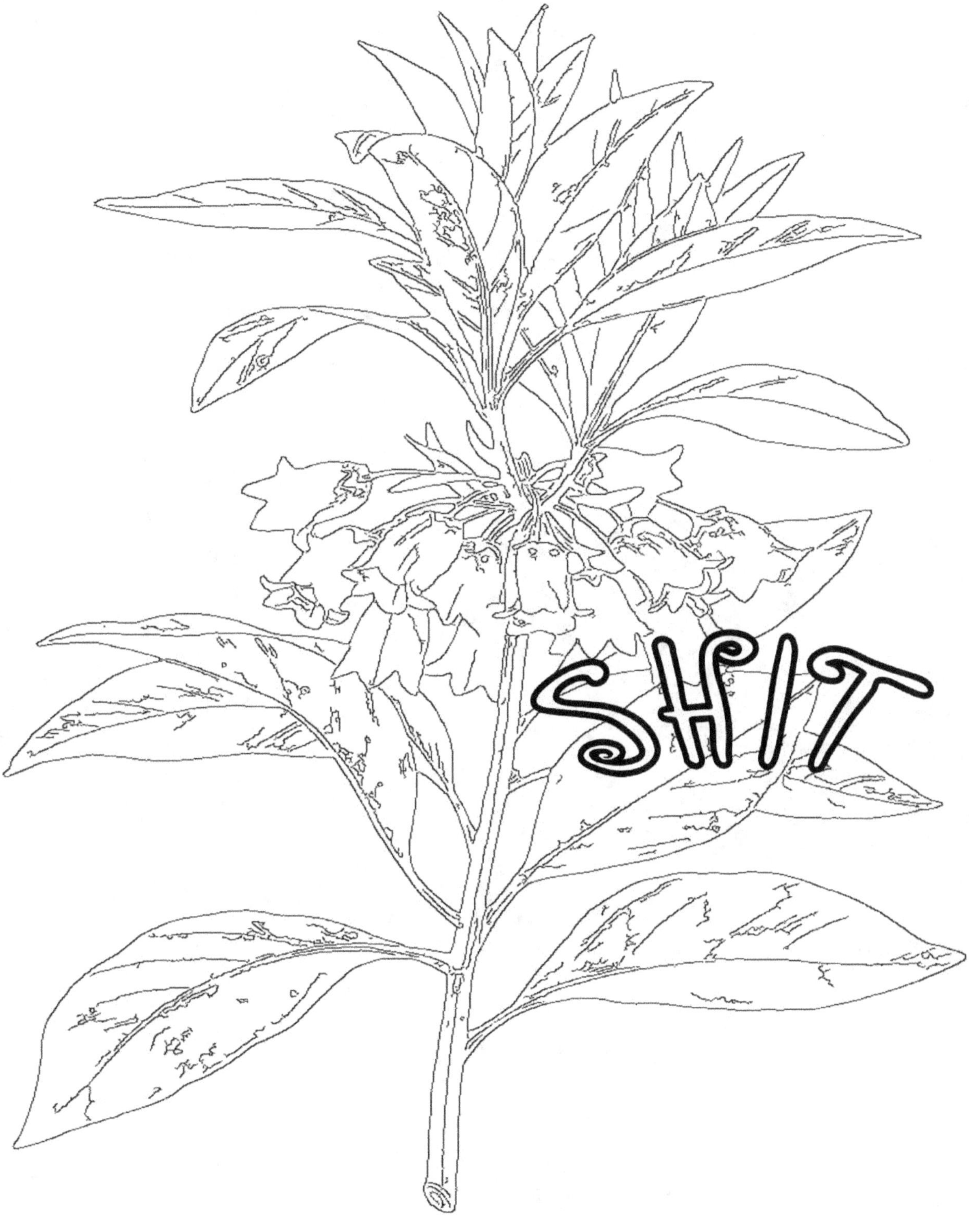
SHIT

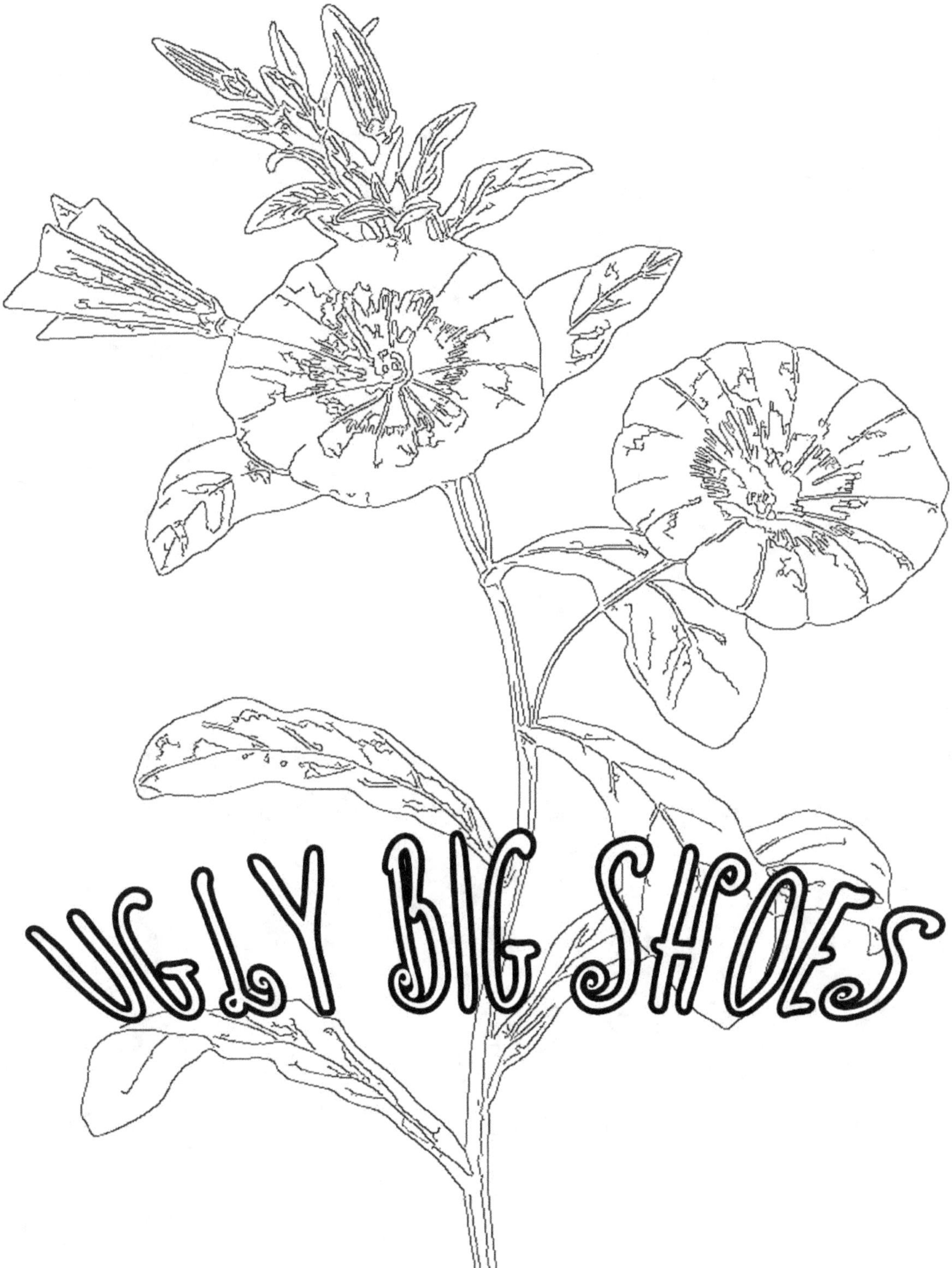
UGLY BIG SHOES

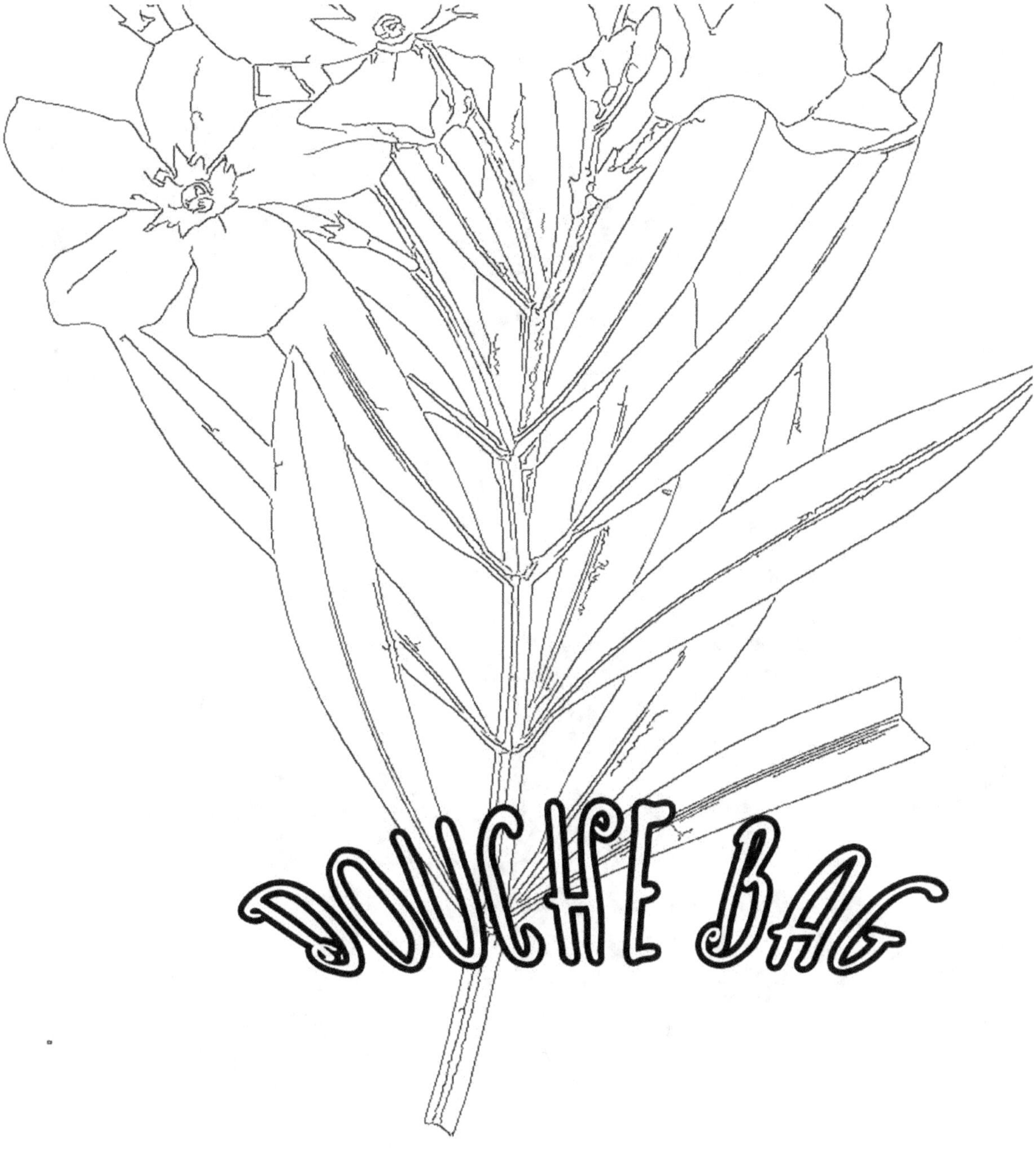
DOUCHE BAG

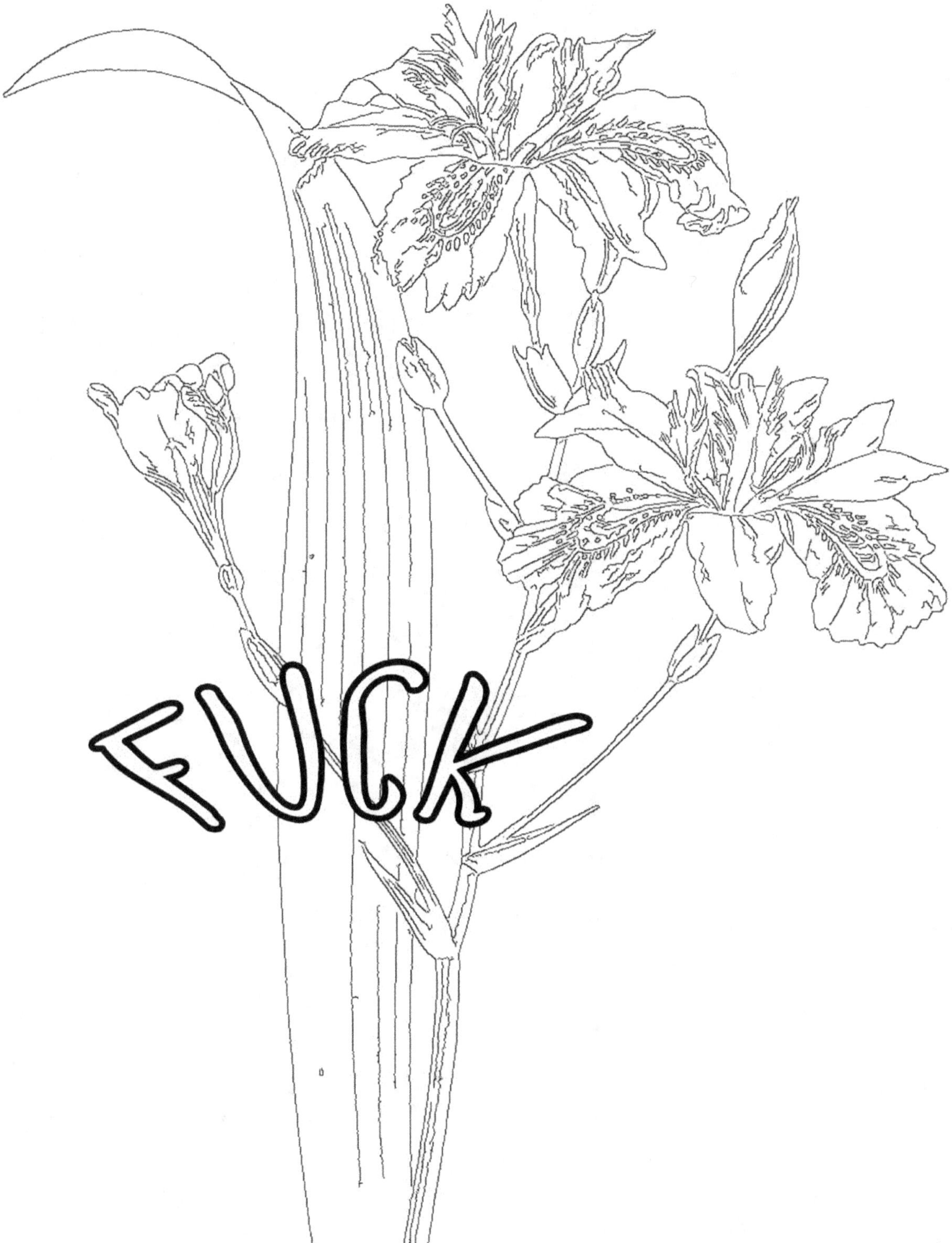
FUCK

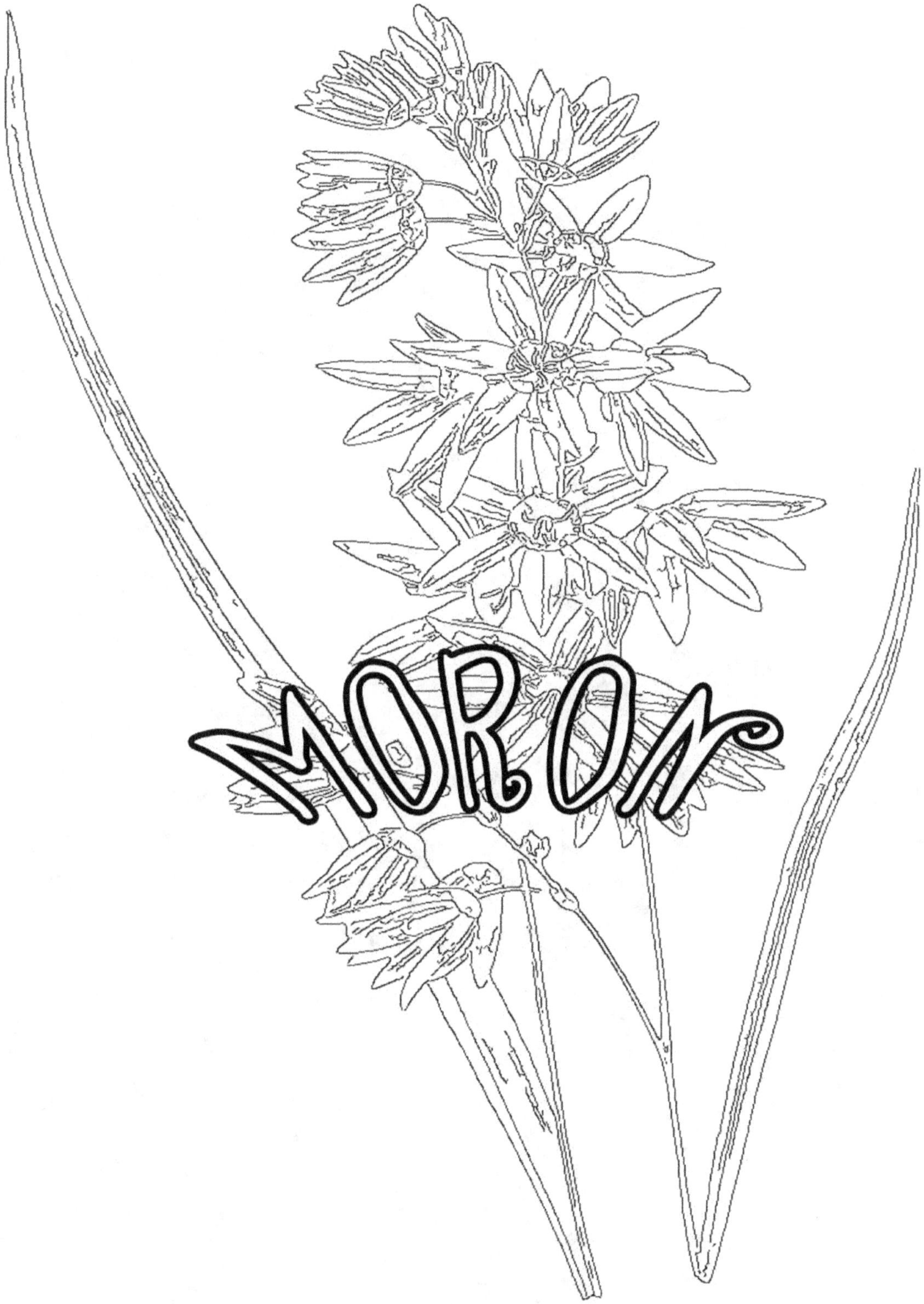
MORON

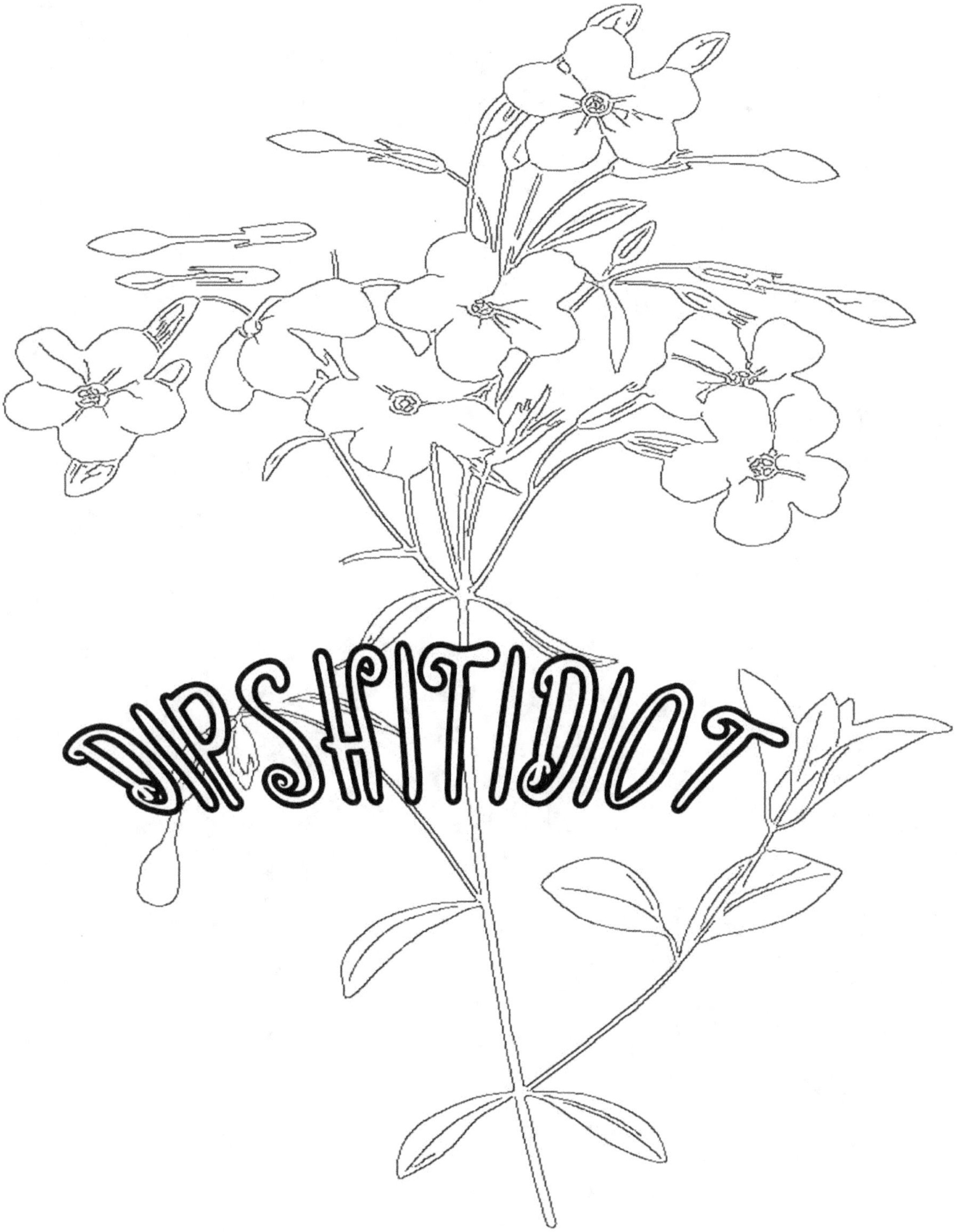
DIPSHITIDIOT

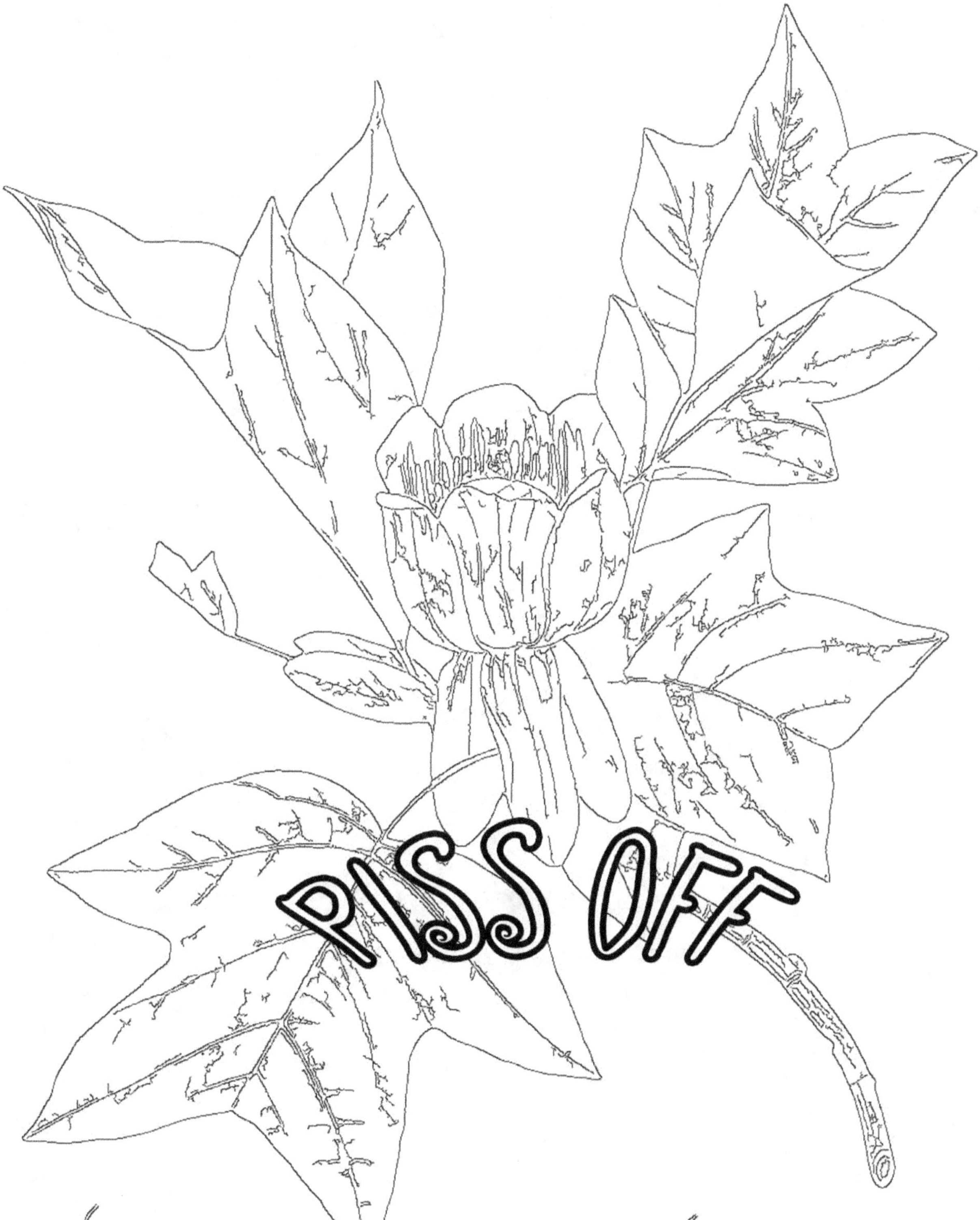
PISS OFF

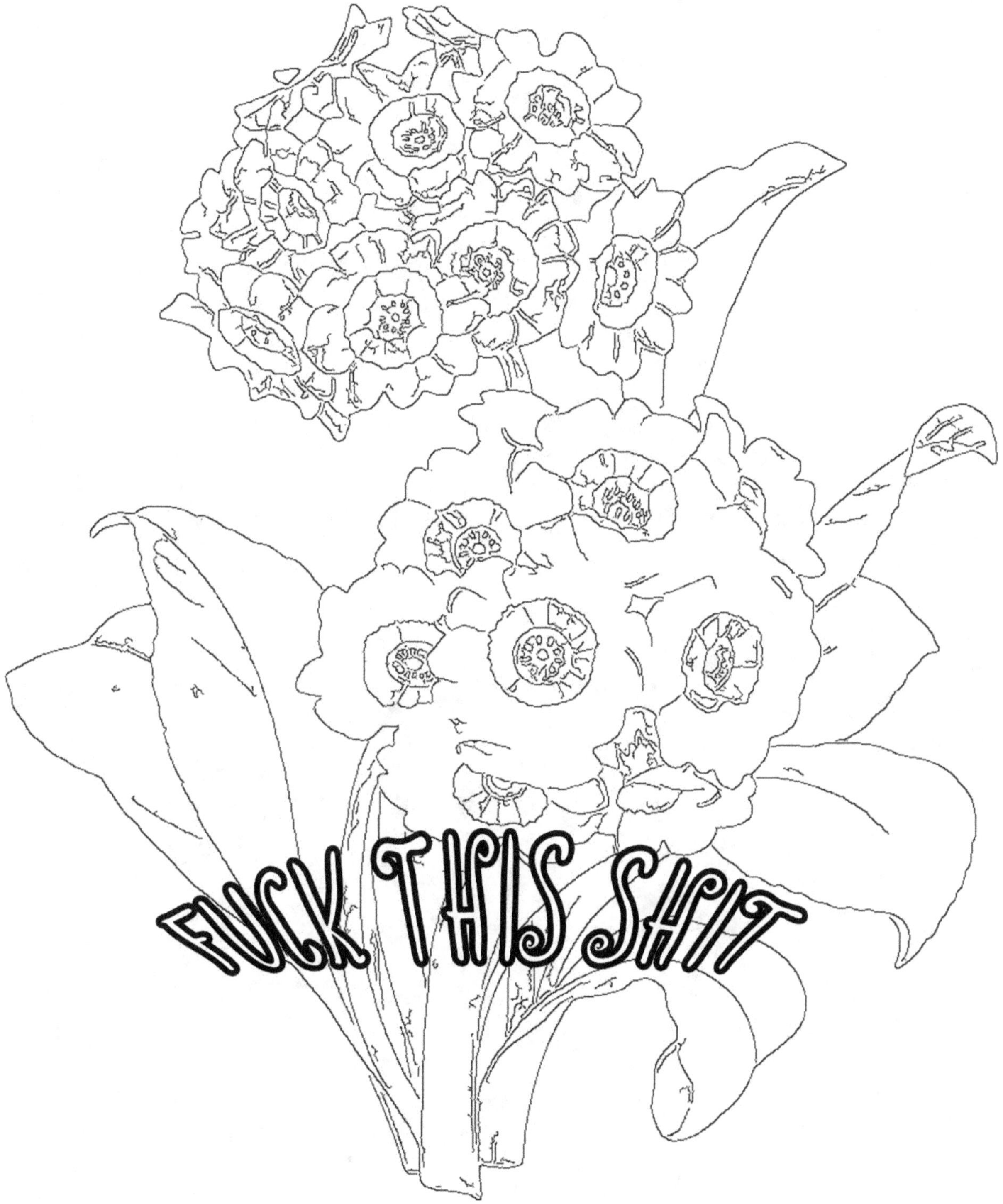
FUCK THIS SHIT

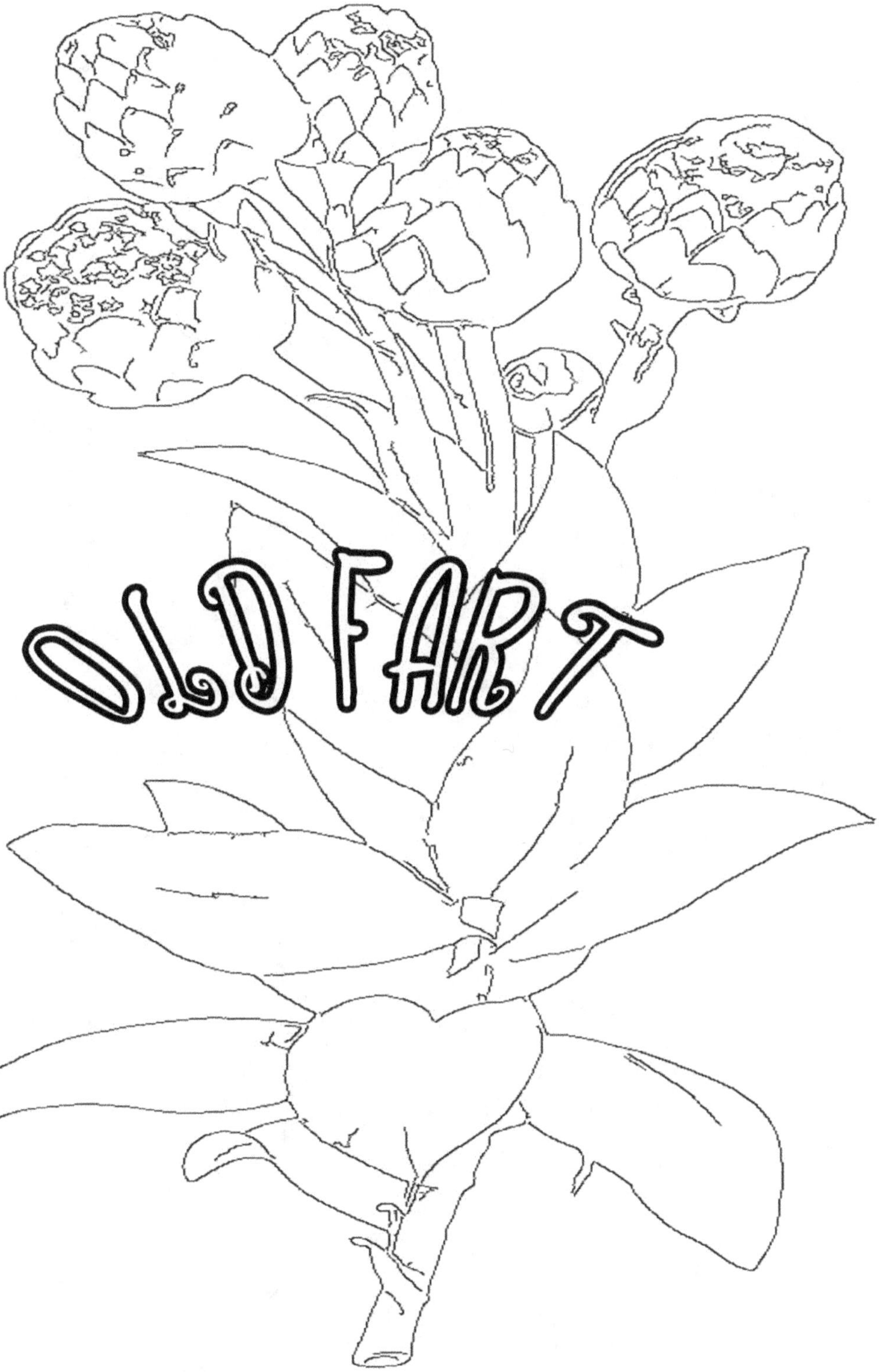
OLD FART

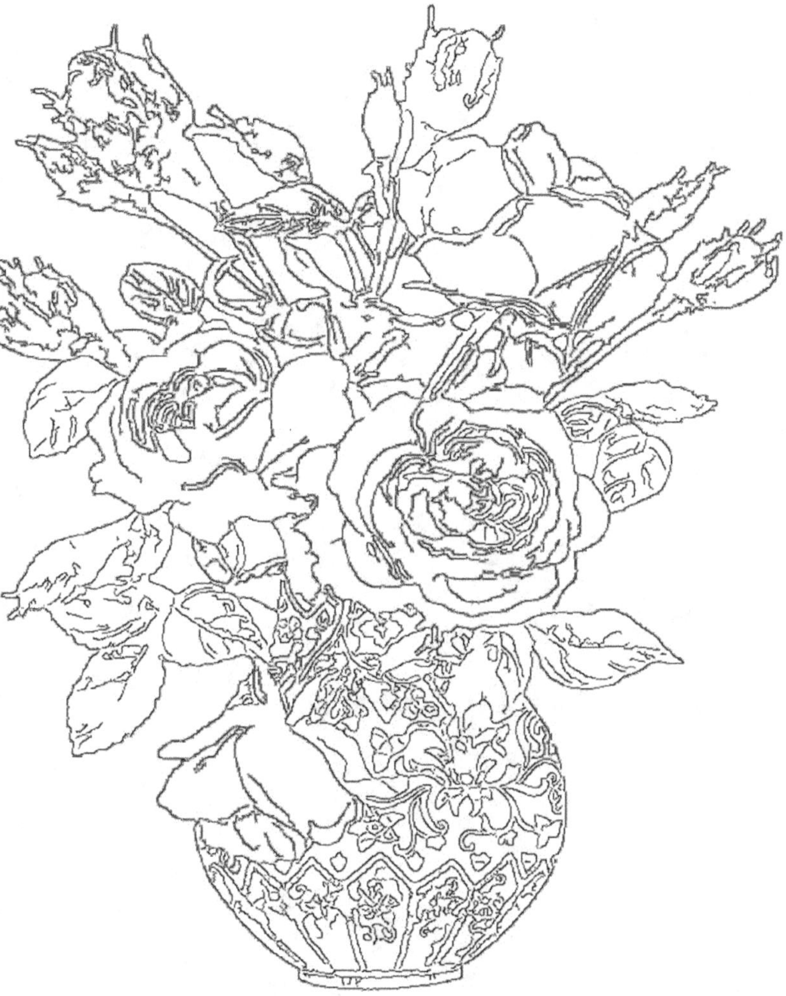

Have a good day.

www.ingramcontent.com/pod-product-compliance
Lightning Source LLC
Chambersburg PA
CBHW081619220526
45468CB00010B/2942
* 9 7 8 1 9 8 3 4 7 1 7 3 5 *